WEEKLY PLANNER

WEEK: **FROM:**

I AM... WORTHY/ LOVED /SUPPORTED/ ENOUGH /ABUNDANT/ PROTECTED/ STRONG/ POWERFUL/ STRONG/ WANTED/ BEAUTIFUL/ TALENTED /CONFIDENT/ FREE / HEALTHY/ CHERISHED/ RESILIENT/ UNSTOPPABLE / INTELLEGENT

REFLECT:

HABITS   M T W T F S S

- *
- *
- *
- *

UPCOMING EVENTS/ OCCASIONS:

THIS WEEK'S PRIORITIES

Plans to do this week

- M
- T
- W
- T
- F
- S
- S

What do you keep forgetting?

What task never seem to get done?

What really worked this week?

What have you been thinking about?

What was the best moment this week?

Notes/Dairy

I AM _____.

DATE

WEATHER M T W T F S S

ENERGY

DO IT TODAY

THINGS I AM GRATEFUL FOR
*
*
*

WATER

PRIORITIES

DO IMMEDIATELY | **DO LATER** | **DELEGATE**

MY ALARMS
*
*
*
*
*
*
*

MAKE
↳
CLEAN
↳
BUY
↳

NOTES/SKETCH

MOOD

Notes/Dairy

I AM _____.

DATE

WEATHER ⚡ ⛅ 🌧️ ❄️ ⛈️ ☁️

M T W T F S S

ENERGY

DO IT TODAY

THINGS I AM GRATEFUL FOR

* _____
* _____
* _____

WATER

PRIORITIES

DO IMMEDIATELY | **DO LATER** | **DELEGATE**

MY ALARMS
* _____
* _____
* _____
* _____
* _____
* _____

MAKE _____
CLEAN _____
BUY _____

NOTES/SKETCH
....
....
....

MOOD

Notes/Dairy

I AM _____.

DATE

WEATHER

M T W T F S S

ENERGY

DO IT TODAY

THINGS I AM GRATEFUL FOR

* _____
* _____
* _____

WATER

PRIORITIES

DO IMMEDIATELY | **DO LATER** | **DELEGATE**

MY ALARMS
* _____
* _____
* _____
* _____
* _____
* _____

MAKE ↳ _____
CLEAN ↳ _____
BUY ↳ _____

NOTES/SKETCH
. . . .
. . . .
. . . .

MOOD

Notes/Dairy

I AM _____.

DATE

WEATHER   M T W T F S S

ENERGY

WATER

DO IT TODAY

THINGS I AM GRATEFUL FOR
*
*
*

PRIORITIES

DO IMMEDIATELY

DO LATER

DELEGATE

MY ALARMS
*
*
*
*
*
*
*

MAKE ↳ _____
CLEAN ↳ _____
BUY ↳ _____

NOTES/SKETCH

MOOD

Notes/Dairy

I AM _____.   DATE

WEATHER ⚡ ⛅ 🌧️ ❄️ ⛈️ ☁️   M T W T F S S

DO IT TODAY

ENERGY

WATER

THINGS I AM GRATEFUL FOR
* _____
* _____
* _____

PRIORITIES

DO IMMEDIATELY | **DO LATER** | **DELEGATE**

MY ALARMS
* _____
* _____
* _____
* _____
* _____
* _____
* _____

MAKE _____
CLEAN _____
BUY _____

NOTES/SKETCH
. . . .
. . . .
. . . .

MOOD

Notes/Dairy

I AM _____.

DATE

WEATHER ⚡ ⛅ 🌧 ❄ ⛈ ☁

Ⓜ Ⓣ Ⓦ Ⓣ Ⓕ Ⓢ Ⓢ

ENERGY

WATER

DO IT TODAY

THINGS I AM GRATEFUL FOR
* _____
* _____
* _____

PRIORITIES

DO IMMEDIATELY

DO LATER

DELEGATE

MY ALARMS
* _____
* _____
* _____
* _____
* _____
* _____
* _____

MAKE _____
CLEAN _____
BUY _____

NOTES/SKETCH

MOOD

Notes/Dairy

I AM_____.   DATE

WEATHER ⚡ ⛅ 🌧️ ❄️ ⛈️ ☁️   M T W T F S S

DO IT TODAY

ENERGY

WATER

THINGS I AM GRATEFUL FOR
*
*
*

PRIORITIES

DO IMMEDIATELY

DO LATER

DELEGATE

MY ALARMS
*
*
*
*
*
*
*

MAKE ↳ _____
CLEAN ↳ _____
BUY ↳ _____

NOTES/SKETCH

MOOD

Notes/Dairy

WEEKLY PLANNER

WEEK: **FROM:** **TO:**

I AM... WORTHY/ LOVED /SUPPORTED/ ENOUGH /ABUNDANT/ PROTECTED/ STRONG/ POWERFUL/ STRONG/ WANTED/ BEAUTIFUL/ TALENTED /CONFIDENT/ FREE / HEALTHY/ CHERISHED/ RESILIENT/ UNSTOPPABLE / INTELLEGENT

REFLECT:

HABITS | M T W T F S S

*
*
*
*

UPCOMING EVENTS/ OCCASIONS:

THIS WEEK'S PRIORITIES

Plans to do this week

- M
- T
- W
- T
- F
- S
- S

What do you keep forgetting?

What task never seem to get done?

What really worked this week?

What have you been thinking about?

What was the best moment this week?

Notes/Dairy

I AM _____.

DATE

WEATHER ⚡ ⛅ 🌧️ ❄️ ⛈️ ☁️

Ⓜ️ Ⓣ Ⓦ Ⓣ Ⓕ Ⓢ Ⓢ

🔋 **ENERGY**

DO IT TODAY

THINGS I AM GRATEFUL FOR

* _____
* _____
* _____

WATER

PRIORITIES

DO IMMEDIATELY | **DO LATER** | **DELEGATE**

MY ALARMS
* _____
* _____
* _____
* _____
* _____
* _____

MAKE ↳ _____
CLEAN ↳ _____
BUY ↳ _____

NOTES/SKETCH
. . . .

MOOD

Notes/Dairy

I AM _____.

DATE

WEATHER

M T W T F S S

ENERGY

WATER

DO IT TODAY

PRIORITIES

THINGS I AM GRATEFUL FOR

*
*
*

DO IMMEDIATELY

DO LATER

DELEGATE

MY ALARMS
*
*
*
*
*
*
*

MAKE
CLEAN
BUY

NOTES/SKETCH

MOOD

Notes/Dairy

I AM _____.   DATE

WEATHER ⚡ ⛅ 🌧 ❄ ⛈ ☁   M T W T F S S

ENERGY

DO IT TODAY

THINGS I AM GRATEFUL FOR
* _____
* _____
* _____

WATER

PRIORITIES

DO IMMEDIATELY | **DO LATER** | **DELEGATE**

MY ALARMS
* _____
* _____
* _____
* _____
* _____
* _____

MAKE _____
CLEAN _____
BUY _____

NOTES/SKETCH

MOOD

Notes/Dairy

I AM _____. DATE

WEATHER M T W T F S S

ENERGY

DO IT TODAY

THINGS I AM GRATEFUL FOR
*
*
*

WATER

PRIORITIES

DO IMMEDIATELY **DO LATER** **DELEGATE**

MY ALARMS
*
*
*
*
*
*

MAKE _____
CLEAN _____
BUY _____

NOTES/SKETCH

MOOD

Notes/Dairy

I AM _____. DATE

WEATHER   M T W T F S S

DO IT TODAY

ENERGY

WATER

THINGS I AM GRATEFUL FOR
* _____
* _____
* _____

PRIORITIES

DO IMMEDIATELY   **DO LATER**   **DELEGATE**

MY ALARMS
* _____
* _____
* _____
* _____
* _____
* _____

MAKE _____
CLEAN _____
BUY _____

NOTES/SKETCH
. . . .
. . . .
. . . .

MOOD

Notes/Dairy

I AM_____.   DATE

WEATHER ⚡ ⛅ 🌧 ❄ ☁ ⛈   M T W T F S S

ENERGY

WATER

DO IT TODAY

THINGS I AM GRATEFUL FOR
*
*
*

PRIORITIES

DO IMMEDIATELY

DO LATER

DELEGATE

MY ALARMS
*
*
*
*
*
*

MAKE ↳_____
CLEAN ↳_____
BUY ↳_____

NOTES/SKETCH
. . . .

MOOD

Notes/Dairy

I AM _____.

DATE

WEATHER

M T W T F S S

ENERGY

WATER

DO IT TODAY

THINGS I AM GRATEFUL FOR
*
*
*

PRIORITIES

DO IMMEDIATELY

DO LATER

DELEGATE

MY ALARMS
*
*
*
*
*
*
*

MAKE ↳
CLEAN ↳
BUY ↳

NOTES/SKETCH

MOOD

Notes/Dairy

WEEKLY PLANNER

WEEK: **FROM:** **TO:**

I AM... WORTHY/ LOVED /SUPPORTED/ ENOUGH /ABUNDANT/ PROTECTED/ STRONG/ POWERFUL/ STRONG/ WANTED/ BEAUTIFUL/ TALENTED /CONFIDENT/ FREE / HEALTHY/ CHERISHED/ RESILIENT/ UNSTOPPABLE / INTELLEGENT

REFLECT:

HABITS

	M	T	W	T	F	S	S

*
*
*
*

UPCOMING EVENTS/ OCCASIONS:

THIS WEEK'S PRIORITIES

Plans to do this week

- M
- T
- W
- T
- F
- S
- S

What do you keep forgetting?

What task never seem to get done?

What really worked this week?

What have you been thinking about?

What was the best moment this week?

Notes/Dairy

I AM_____. DATE

WEATHER

M T W T F S S

ENERGY

WATER

DO IT TODAY

PRIORITIES

THINGS I AM GRATEFUL FOR
*
*
*

DO IMMEDIATELY

DO LATER

DELEGATE

MY ALARMS
*
*
*
*
*
*
*

MAKE
CLEAN
BUY

NOTES/SKETCH

MOOD

Notes/Dairy

I AM _____.

DATE

WEATHER   M T W T F S S

ENERGY

WATER

DO IT TODAY

THINGS I AM GRATEFUL FOR
* _____
* _____
* _____

PRIORITIES

DO IMMEDIATELY | **DO LATER** | **DELEGATE**

MY ALARMS
* _____
* _____
* _____
* _____
* _____
* _____
* _____

MAKE ↳ _____
CLEAN ↳ _____
BUY ↳ _____

NOTES/SKETCH
....
....
....

MOOD

Notes/Dairy

I AM _____.

DATE

WEATHER

M T W T F S S

ENERGY

DO IT TODAY

THINGS I AM GRATEFUL FOR
* _____
* _____
* _____

WATER

PRIORITIES

DO IMMEDIATELY | **DO LATER** | **DELEGATE**

MY ALARMS
* _____
* _____
* _____
* _____
* _____
* _____
* _____

MAKE ↳ _____
CLEAN ↳ _____
BUY ↳ _____

NOTES/SKETCH

MOOD

Notes/Dairy

I AM _____.

DATE

WEATHER

M T W T F S S

ENERGY

WATER

DO IT TODAY

THINGS I AM GRATEFUL FOR
* _____
* _____
* _____

PRIORITIES

DO IMMEDIATELY

DO LATER

DELEGATE

MY ALARMS
* _____
* _____
* _____
* _____
* _____
* _____

MAKE ↳ _____
CLEAN ↳ _____
BUY ↳ _____

NOTES/SKETCH

MOOD

Notes/Dairy

I AM _____.

DATE

WEATHER

M T W T F S S

ENERGY

WATER

DO IT TODAY

THINGS I AM GRATEFUL FOR
* _____
* _____
* _____

PRIORITIES

DO IMMEDIATELY

DO LATER

DELEGATE

MY ALARMS
* _____
* _____
* _____
* _____
* _____
* _____
* _____

MAKE
↳ _____
CLEAN
↳ _____
BUY
↳ _____

NOTES/SKETCH

MOOD

Notes/Dairy

I AM _____.

DATE

WEATHER

M T W T F S S

ENERGY

WATER

DO IT TODAY

THINGS I AM GRATEFUL FOR

*
*
*

PRIORITIES

DO IMMEDIATELY

DO LATER

DELEGATE

MY ALARMS
*
*
*
*
*
*

MAKE
CLEAN
BUY

NOTES/SKETCH

MOOD

Notes/Dairy

I AM _____.

DATE

WEATHER

M T W T F S S

ENERGY

WATER

DO IT TODAY

THINGS I AM GRATEFUL FOR
* _____
* _____
* _____

PRIORITIES

DO IMMEDIATELY

DO LATER

DELEGATE

MY ALARMS
* _____
* _____
* _____
* _____
* _____
* _____

MAKE
↳ _____

CLEAN
↳ _____

BUY
↳ _____

NOTES/SKETCH

MOOD

Notes/Dairy

WEEKLY PLANNER

WEEK: **FROM:** **TO:**

I AM... WORTHY/ LOVED /SUPPORTED/ ENOUGH /ABUNDANT/ PROTECTED/ STRONG/ POWERFUL/ STRONG/ WANTED/ BEAUTIFUL/ TALENTED /CONFIDENT/ FREE / HEALTHY/ CHERISHED/ RESILIENT/ UNSTOPPABLE / INTELLEGENT

REFLECT:

HABITS — M T W T F S S

*
*
*
*

UPCOMING EVENTS/ OCCASIONS:

THIS WEEK'S PRIORITIES

Plans to do this week

M
T
W
T
F
S
S

- What do you keep forgetting?
- What task never seem to get done?
- What really worked this week?
- What have you been thinking about?
- What was the best moment this week?

Notes/Dairy

I AM _____.

DATE

WEATHER

M T W T F S S

ENERGY

DO IT TODAY

THINGS I AM GRATEFUL FOR

* _____
* _____
* _____

WATER

PRIORITIES

DO IMMEDIATELY

DO LATER

DELEGATE

MY ALARMS
* _____
* _____
* _____
* _____
* _____
* _____

MAKE
↳ _____
CLEAN
↳ _____
BUY
↳ _____

NOTES/SKETCH
. . . .

MOOD

Notes/Dairy

I AM _____.

DATE

WEATHER M T W T F S S

ENERGY

WATER

DO IT TODAY

THINGS I AM GRATEFUL FOR
* _____
* _____
* _____

PRIORITIES

DO IMMEDIATELY

DO LATER

DELEGATE

MY ALARMS
* _____
* _____
* _____
* _____
* _____
* _____

MAKE ↳ _____
CLEAN ↳ _____
BUY ↳ _____

NOTES/SKETCH
. . . .

MOOD

Notes/Dairy

I AM _____. DATE

WEATHER ⚡ ⛅ 🌧 ❄ ⛈ ☁ Ⓜ Ⓣ Ⓦ Ⓣ Ⓕ Ⓢ Ⓢ

ENERGY

DO IT TODAY

THINGS I AM GRATEFUL FOR
* _____
* _____
* _____

WATER

PRIORITIES

DO IMMEDIATELY **DO LATER** **DELEGATE**

MY ALARMS
* _____
* _____
* _____
* _____
* _____

MAKE ↳ _____
CLEAN ↳ _____
BUY ↳ _____

NOTES/SKETCH
. . . .

MOOD

Notes/Dairy

I AM _____.

DATE

WEATHER M T W T F S S

ENERGY

WATER

DO IT TODAY

THINGS I AM GRATEFUL FOR
*
*
*

PRIORITIES

DO IMMEDIATELY

DO LATER

DELEGATE

MY ALARMS
*
*
*
*
*
*

MAKE ↳ _____
CLEAN ↳ _____
BUY ↳ _____

NOTES/SKETCH
. . . .
. . . .
. . . .

MOOD

Notes/Dairy

I AM _____.

DATE

WEATHER

M T W T F S S

ENERGY

WATER

DO IT TODAY

THINGS I AM GRATEFUL FOR

* _____
* _____
* _____

PRIORITIES

DO IMMEDIATELY

DO LATER

DELEGATE

MY ALARMS
* _____
* _____
* _____
* _____
* _____
* _____

MAKE ↳ _____
CLEAN ↳ _____
BUY ↳ _____

NOTES/SKETCH
. . . .
. . . .
. . . .

MOOD

Notes/Dairy

I AM _____.

DATE

WEATHER

M T W T F S S

ENERGY

WATER

DO IT TODAY

PRIORITIES

THINGS I AM GRATEFUL FOR
*
*
*

DO IMMEDIATELY

DO LATER

DELEGATE

MY ALARMS
*
*
*
*
*
*
*

MAKE ↳ _____
CLEAN ↳ _____
BUY ↳ _____

NOTES/SKETCH

MOOD

Notes/Dairy

I AM _____.

DATE

WEATHER M T W T F S S

ENERGY

WATER

DO IT TODAY

PRIORITIES

THINGS I AM GRATEFUL FOR
* _____
* _____
* _____

DO IMMEDIATELY

DO LATER

DELEGATE

MY ALARMS
* _____
* _____
* _____
* _____
* _____
* _____

MAKE ↳ _____
CLEAN ↳ _____
BUY ↳ _____

NOTES/SKETCH

MOOD

Notes/Dairy

WEEKLY PLANNER

WEEK: **FROM:** **TO:**

I AM... WORTHY/ LOVED /SUPPORTED/ ENOUGH /ABUNDANT/ PROTECTED/ STRONG/ POWERFUL/ STRONG/ WANTED/ BEAUTIFUL/ TALENTED /CONFIDENT/ FREE / HEALTHY/ CHERISHED/ RESILIENT/ UNSTOPPABLE / INTELLEGENT

REFLECT:

HABITS

	M	T	W	T	F	S	S

* _____
* _____
* _____
* _____

UPCOMING EVENTS/ OCCASIONS:

THIS WEEK'S PRIORITIES

Plans to do this week

M	
T	
W	
T	
F	
S	
S	

What do you keep forgetting?

What task never seem to get done?

What really worked this week?

What have you been thinking about?

What was the best moment this week?

Notes/Dairy

I AM _____.

DATE

WEATHER

M T W T F S S

ENERGY

DO IT TODAY

THINGS I AM GRATEFUL FOR
*
*
*

WATER

PRIORITIES

DO IMMEDIATELY

DO LATER

DELEGATE

MY ALARMS
*
*
*
*
*
*
*

MAKE ↳ _____
CLEAN ↳ _____
BUY ↳ _____

NOTES/SKETCH

MOOD

Notes/Dairy

I AM _____.

DATE

WEATHER M T W T F S S

ENERGY

WATER

DO IT TODAY

THINGS I AM GRATEFUL FOR
* _____
* _____
* _____

PRIORITIES

DO IMMEDIATELY

DO LATER

DELEGATE

MY ALARMS
* _____
* _____
* _____
* _____
* _____
* _____

MAKE ↳ _____
CLEAN ↳ _____
BUY ↳ _____

NOTES/SKETCH
....
....
....

MOOD

Notes/Dairy

I AM _____.

DATE

WEATHER

M T W T F S S

ENERGY

WATER

DO IT TODAY

THINGS I AM GRATEFUL FOR
* _____
* _____
* _____

PRIORITIES

DO IMMEDIATELY

DO LATER

DELEGATE

MY ALARMS
* _____
* _____
* _____
* _____
* _____
* _____

MAKE _____
CLEAN _____
BUY _____

NOTES/SKETCH

MOOD

Notes/Dairy

I AM _____.

DATE

WEATHER

M T W T F S S

ENERGY

WATER

DO IT TODAY

THINGS I AM GRATEFUL FOR
* _____
* _____
* _____

PRIORITIES

DO IMMEDIATELY

DO LATER

DELEGATE

MY ALARMS
* _____
* _____
* _____
* _____
* _____
* _____

MAKE ↳ _____
CLEAN ↳ _____
BUY ↳ _____

NOTES/SKETCH

MOOD

Notes/Dairy

I AM _____.

DATE

WEATHER ⚡ ⛅ 🌧️ ❄️ ⛈️ ☁️ Ⓜ Ⓣ Ⓦ Ⓣ Ⓕ Ⓢ Ⓢ

ENERGY 🔋

🍷🍷🍷🍷
🍷🍷🍷🍷

WATER

DO IT TODAY

🦷 🩺 📚 🚗 🐕 🚿
🧺 🏠✨ 🪣🧹 ✉️ 🎨 🧘

THINGS I AM GRATEFUL FOR

* _____
* _____
* _____

PRIORITIES

DO IMMEDIATELY	DO LATER	DELEGATE

MY ALARMS ⏰
* _____
* _____
* _____
* _____
* _____
* _____

MAKE ↳ _____
CLEAN ↳ _____
BUY ↳ _____

NOTES/SKETCH

. . . .

MOOD 😳 🥺 😈 😍 ☹️ 😓 😔 🙄 😟 😧 😭 🤔 😊

Notes/Dairy

I AM _____.

DATE

WEATHER

M T W T F S S

ENERGY

DO IT TODAY

WATER

THINGS I AM GRATEFUL FOR

* _____
* _____
* _____

PRIORITIES

DO IMMEDIATELY
DO LATER
DELEGATE

MY ALARMS
* _____
* _____
* _____
* _____
* _____
* _____
* _____

MAKE
↳ _____

CLEAN
↳ _____

BUY
↳ _____

NOTES/SKETCH

MOOD

Notes/Dairy

I AM _____.

DATE

WEATHER M T W T F S S

ENERGY

WATER

DO IT TODAY

THINGS I AM GRATEFUL FOR
*
*
*

PRIORITIES

DO IMMEDIATELY

DO LATER

DELEGATE

MY ALARMS
*
*
*
*
*
*

MAKE ↳ _____
CLEAN ↳ _____
BUY ↳ _____

NOTES/SKETCH

MOOD

Notes/Dairy

WEEKLY PLANNER

WEEK: **FROM:** **TO:**

I AM... WORTHY/ LOVED /SUPPORTED/ ENOUGH /ABUNDANT/ PROTECTED/ STRONG/ POWERFUL/ STRONG/ WANTED/ BEAUTIFUL/ TALENTED /CONFIDENT/ FREE / HEALTHY/ CHERISHED/ RESILIENT/ UNSTOPPABLE / INTELLEGENT

REFLECT:

HABITS — M T W T F S S

* _____
* _____
* _____
* _____

UPCOMING EVENTS/ OCCASIONS:

THIS WEEK'S PRIORITIES

Plans to do this week

- M
- T
- W
- T
- F
- S
- S

- What do you keep forgetting?
- What task never seem to get done?
- What really worked this week?
- What have you been thinking about?
- What was the best moment this week?

Notes/Dairy

I AM _____.

DATE

WEATHER

M T W T F S S

ENERGY

WATER

DO IT TODAY

THINGS I AM GRATEFUL FOR
* _____
* _____
* _____

PRIORITIES

DO IMMEDIATELY

DO LATER

DELEGATE

MY ALARMS
* _____
* _____
* _____
* _____
* _____
* _____

MAKE _____
CLEAN _____
BUY _____

NOTES/SKETCH

MOOD

Notes/Dairy

I AM _____.

DATE

WEATHER

(M)(T)(W)(T)(F)(S)(S)

ENERGY

WATER

DO IT TODAY

THINGS I AM GRATEFUL FOR
* _____
* _____
* _____

PRIORITIES

DO IMMEDIATELY

DO LATER

DELEGATE

MY ALARMS
* _____
* _____
* _____
* _____
* _____
* _____

MAKE _____
CLEAN _____
BUY _____

NOTES/SKETCH

MOOD

Notes/Dairy

I AM_____.

DATE

WEATHER ⚡ ⛅ 🌧 ❄ ⛈ ☁

(M) (T) (W) (T) (F) (S) (S)

ENERGY

🔋

WATER
🍷🍷🍷🍷
🍷🍷🍷🍷

DO IT TODAY
🦷 🩺 📚 🚗 🐕 🚿
🧺 🏠 🧹 ✉ 🎨 🧘

THINGS I AM GRATEFUL FOR
* _____
* _____
* _____

PRIORITIES

DO IMMEDIATELY | **DO LATER** | **DELEGATE**

MY ALARMS ⏰
* _____
* _____
* _____
* _____
* _____
* _____

MAKE ↳ _____
CLEAN ↳ _____
BUY ↳ _____

NOTES/SKETCH
. . . .
. . . .
. . . .

MOOD 😀 🥺 😈 😍 ☹ 😌 😟 🙄 😦 😮 😭 😗 😊

Notes/Dairy

I AM _____.

DATE

WEATHER

M T W T F S S

ENERGY

WATER

DO IT TODAY

THINGS I AM GRATEFUL FOR
* _____
* _____
* _____

PRIORITIES

DO IMMEDIATELY

DO LATER

DELEGATE

MY ALARMS
* _____
* _____
* _____
* _____
* _____
* _____
* _____

MAKE
↳ _____
CLEAN
↳ _____
BUY
↳ _____

NOTES/SKETCH

MOOD

Notes/Dairy

I AM _____.

DATE

WEATHER ⚡ ⛅ 🌧 ❄ ⛈ ☁

M T W T F S S

ENERGY

WATER

DO IT TODAY

THINGS I AM GRATEFUL FOR
*
*
*

PRIORITIES

DO IMMEDIATELY
DO LATER
DELEGATE

MY ALARMS
*
*
*
*
*
*

MAKE ↳ _____
CLEAN ↳ _____
BUY ↳ _____

NOTES/SKETCH

MOOD

Notes/Dairy

I AM _____.

DATE

WEATHER M T W T F S S

ENERGY

WATER

DO IT TODAY

THINGS I AM GRATEFUL FOR
* _____
* _____
* _____

PRIORITIES

DO IMMEDIATELY

DO LATER

DELEGATE

MY ALARMS
* _____
* _____
* _____
* _____
* _____
* _____

MAKE
↳ _____
CLEAN
↳ _____
BUY
↳ _____

NOTES/SKETCH

MOOD

Notes/Dairy

I AM_____.   DATE

WEATHER   ⚡ ⛅ 🌧 ❄ ⛈ ☁   Ⓜ Ⓣ Ⓦ Ⓣ Ⓕ Ⓢ Ⓢ

ENERGY

WATER

DO IT TODAY

THINGS I AM GRATEFUL FOR
* _____
* _____
* _____

PRIORITIES

DO IMMEDIATELY | **DO LATER** | **DELEGATE**

MY ALARMS
* _____
* _____
* _____
* _____
* _____
* _____

MAKE
↳ _____
CLEAN
↳ _____
BUY
↳ _____

NOTES/SKETCH
. . . .

MOOD

Notes/Dairy

WEEKLY PLANNER

WEEK: **FROM:** **TO:**

I AM... WORTHY/ LOVED /SUPPORTED/ ENOUGH /ABUNDANT/ PROTECTED/ STRONG/ POWERFUL/ STRONG/ WANTED/ BEAUTIFUL/ TALENTED /CONFIDENT/ FREE / HEALTHY/ CHERISHED/ RESILIENT/ UNSTOPPABLE / INTELLEGENT

REFLECT:

HABITS | M T W T F S S

* _____
* _____
* _____
* _____

UPCOMING EVENTS/ OCCASIONS:

THIS WEEK'S PRIORITIES

Plans to do this week

- M
- T
- W
- T
- F
- S
- S

What do you keep forgetting?

What task never seem to get done?

What really worked this week?

What have you been thinking about?

What was the best moment this week?

Notes/Dairy

I AM _____.

DATE

WEATHER ⚡ ⛅ 🌧 ❄ ⛈ ☁

M T W T F S S

ENERGY

WATER

DO IT TODAY

PRIORITIES

THINGS I AM GRATEFUL FOR
* _____
* _____
* _____

DO IMMEDIATELY | **DO LATER** | **DELEGATE**

MY ALARMS
* _____
* _____
* _____
* _____
* _____
* _____

MAKE ↳ _____
CLEAN ↳ _____
BUY ↳ _____

NOTES/SKETCH
. . . .
. . . .
. . . .

MOOD

Notes/Dairy

I AM _____.

DATE

WEATHER

M T W T F S S

ENERGY

DO IT TODAY

THINGS I AM GRATEFUL FOR
* _____
* _____
* _____

WATER

PRIORITIES

DO IMMEDIATELY | DO LATER | DELEGATE

MY ALARMS
* _____
* _____
* _____
* _____
* _____
* _____

MAKE ↳ _____
CLEAN ↳ _____
BUY ↳ _____

NOTES/SKETCH

MOOD

Notes/Dairy

Manufactured by Amazon.ca
Bolton, ON

31404121R00068